T0266192

BEGINNINGS

POEMS OF
LIFE AND LOVE

KATHRYN CAROLE ELLISON

Published by Lady Bug Books, an imprint of Brisance Books Group.
Lady Bug Press and the distinctive ladybug logo are registered trademarks of
Lady Bug Books, LLC.

Lady Bug Books
400 112th Avenue N.E.
Suite 230
Bellevue, WA 98004
www.GiftsOfLove.com

For information about custom editions, special sales and permissions, please email
Info@GiftsOfLove.com

Manufactured in the United States of America
ISBN: 978-1-944194-69-7

First Edition: May 2020

A NOTE FROM THE AUTHOR

The poems in this book were written over many years as gifts to my children. I began writing them in the 1970s, when they were reaching the age of reason. And, as I found myself in the position of becoming a single parent, I wanted to do something special to share with them—something that would become a tradition, a ritual they could count on.

And so the Advent Poems began—one day, decades ago—with a poem 'gifted' to them each day during the Advent period leading up to Christmas, December 1 to December 24. Forty some years later... my children still look forward each year to the poems that started a family tradition, that new generations have come to cherish.

It is my sincere hope that you will embrace and enjoy them, and share them with those you love.

Children of the Light was among the early poems I wrote, and is included in each of the *Poems of Life and Love* books in The Ellison Collection: *Heartstrings, Celebrations, Inspirations, Sanctuary, Awakenings, Sojourns, Milestones, Tapestry, Gratitude, Beginnings, Horizons* and *Moments*. After writing many hundreds of poems, it is still my favorite. The words came from my heart... and my soul... and flowed so effortlessly that it was written in a single sitting.
All I needed to do was capture the words on paper.

Light, to me, represented all that was good and pure and right with the world, and I believed then—as I do today—that those elements live in my children, and perhaps in all of us.
We need only to dare.

– KCE

DEDICATION

To my parents: Herb and Bernice Haas

Mom, you were the poet who went before me...
unpublished, but appreciated nonetheless.

And Dad, you always believed in me,
no matter what direction my life took.
Thank you for your faith in me,
and for your unconditional love.

TABLE OF CONTENTS

LIFE'S JOYS

LIFE'S LESSONS

LIFE'S GIFTS

LIFE'S JOYS

ANTICIPATION

If you're coming to see me at four o'clock,
I'll begin to be happy by three.
I'm anticipating your visit, imagining the rush
Of happiness as it pours over me!

Waiting for something good that will happen
Makes it ever more exciting, I find.
The expectation of happiness is happiness itself,
And the time spent waiting? I don't mind.

Pleasure is fun, first in anticipation;
And, after the fact, lies in memory.
Anticipation of a thing is born of hope;
The actual happening completes the story.

We cannot feel good about an imaginary future
When we're feeling bad about an actual present.
Don't underestimate the power of anticipation.
An invitation into the future will bring enjoyment.

There are two ways to face the future:
One with apprehension; the other, anticipation.
The choice is yours: to experience new possibilities,
Or to worry about the outcome with trepidation.

LISTEN WITHIN WITH LOVE

Your child within must be listened to,
Not quieted or ignored by you.
That child is closer to your truth.
The Source is nearest to the youth.

When you listen, judge not the story.
Do not take your "child's" inventory.
Listen patiently with an open heart
And find your truth. You've made a start.

SEPARATENESS IS AN ILLUSION

Mankind suffers an illness
Of the illusion of separateness.
We believe the world is made up
Of discrete things which don't coalesce.
Nothing could be further from the truth.
We are one interconnected whole
In the natural order of things.
It's as if we have but one soul.
We are part of the natural order,
And it's laws are our laws, too.
We are an endless moving stream
In a stream that is endless and true.
All distinctions are falsely imagined.
Separateness is a sickness, to be sure.
We are the eternal mind of the universe,
And Love is the cure.

CHANGING YOURSELF

Changing one's self instead of trying
To change the other person or thing
Is the secret to success in living one's life.
It puts all one's troubles to wing.

Life will constantly pound on you from
The outside with situations and events;
But you have the last word as to how you'll react,
Whether realized and accepting, or tense.

William James once said that the great revelation
Of his generation was the discovery
That human beings, by changing their demeanor,
Could control and change their own destiny.

You cannot climb a hill when thinking about falling down.
Substitute new habits for old.
Make friends with people who are moving up,
And don't always do what you're told.

Let go of lower things and reach for the higher;
You deserve all the good you can find.
Change is realized through conscious evolution.
You become what you hold in your mind.

EXCITEMENT

The joy and excitement of doing what you love
Is what drives you... what keeps you on the path.
The creative habit... the thrill of your creation...
Sets the formula for your success. (Do the math!)

It's said the excitement of learning new things
Will separate youth from old age.
You won't get "old" as long as you keep learning.
Stay curious and excited! Enjoy the voyage.

Get excited and enthusiastic about your own dream.
(This excitement can be compared to a forest fire.
You can smell it, taste it; see it from a mile away.)
Feed your dream with excitement and you will inspire.

Without dreaming, or leaps of imagination,
You will lose the excitement of all the possibilities.
Dreaming can be defined as a form of planning.
With excitement and planning, success is an inevitability.

GIVE BIRTH TO YOURSELF EVERY DAY

Old habits are for old people, so it's said.
So reinvent yourself while you still can.
Each night, as you sleep, you leave it all behind.
Every day is your chance to begin again.

Like the butterfly, you'll go through stages of change,
Be reborn and transform into your new self.
You will create a new clarity of purpose,
And put your outdated ideas back on the shelf.

You'll break out of your comfort zone, to be sure,
And shed old layers of obsolete behavior.
You'll stretch in your potential to be your best self.
Stay on your path. Don't even waver!

Your goal is to be free of outdated limitations.
You'll experience rebirth and take flight.
Follow your dream and pursue your bliss.
Each day is a new life to relish and delight!

DREAMS

Every great dream begins with a dreamer;
And the future belongs to those who can dream.
As long as you can dream, you will have hope.
With hope there's joy in living, it would seem.

Dreams are today's answers to tomorrow's questions.
They're possible to achieve... without fear of failure.
You're never too old to set another goal.
Your dreams know the way! Life is an adventure!

To achieve anything requires faith, and belief in yourself,
Along with vision, hard work and determination.
You have courage to dare to bring your dreams to reality.
Remember: Hope lies in dreams, so use your imagination.

Do not wait! The timing will never be "just right!"
Start from where you are with what tools you have at hand.
Don't let anyone or anything limit your dreams.
Your future will thank you! You are in command!

You don't have to see the whole staircase before you.
Just take the first step and be led by your heart.
Daring to dream means daring to live...
Reach for the stars; change the world. Here is where you start.

CHILDREN OF THE LIGHT

There are those souls who bring the light,
Who spill it out for all to share.
And with a joy that does excite,
They show the world that they do care.
It is so very bright.

In this sharing, love does pervade
Into their lives and cycles round;
And as this light is outward played
The love is also inward bound.
It is an awesome trade.

You are a soul whose light is shared.
It comes from deep within your heart.
It's best because it is not spared,
Because it's total, not just part.
And I am glad you've dared.

CHOICES

Making choices every day is not so hard to do.
Although, I guess, it all depends upon your point of view.
Choices come two different ways, and you must recognize
There is a subtle difference. Thus, I will familiarize.

The first's a choice that you would make for just yourself alone.
The other one you choose to have made for you; you condone.
The thought that's represented is your need to know the difference
So you're in charge to handle any following occurrence.

All your choices, good or bad, have the power to be momentous.
It's a privilege and a burden, with results most often joyous.
You cannot opt to not make a choice, because choosing not to choose
Is, in itself, a choice you make. (I mean not to confuse.)

Remember this about the choices with which you might be faced:
Choice looks to the future, not the past, and should be heartily embraced.
It may seem odd, it may take time and feel a little strange,
But as long as you have the power to choose, you have the
power to change.

GET IN THE GAME

Each one of you must play your own hand
With the cards of life you are dealt.
And, it's up to you to decide how to play.
You must make sure your efforts are felt.

The game of life has its ups and downs,
And you must never lose focus of the goal.
By keeping up the effort you will not falter.
Playing the game is your most important role.

Every day is a new opportunity to build
On yesterday's progress, or start anew.
It's up to you to keep your game going,
As you discover new ways to pursue.

Risk is always a part of the game.
There's no progress or growth without it.
You don't get in the game to test the waters;
You do it to make waves; there's no doubt about it.

Get out of the bleachers, and into the game.
You are a product of your decisions.
The right things will happen if you do your best,
Staying on track to fulfill your visions.

Success is a game of chance; you have control.
There's nobody else you can blame.
You cannot change the cards you're dealt;
You can change only how you play the game.

FAMILY

"The Human Family" voices sing;
It's a good phrase and easy to comprehend.
And, at the holidays, it makes us think.
We come from the same beginning,
And we're headed towards the same end;
And all the while our lives interlink.

A famine in one part of the sphere
Affects all people in all places.
There is no way to be an island.
An assassination in Dallas or Kassimir
Is felt by all as one of life's disgraces.
Our interdependency we must understand.

But families have a way of being islands –
The O'Reilleys as distinct from family Meyer;
And don't confuse them with the French Marchants.
Within each wall each family drama expands –
The births, the deaths, the weddings all transpire;
Other neighbors all pitch in to fill their wants.

It's not that things do happen in a family,
But that the family is the things that happen to it.
The family becomes the total of its experiences –
Every birth or death or every word set free;
Every leaving or return, every house we inhabit;
It's every obvious happening or inadvertence.

A family is a web so delicately woven
That it can break and tear to pieces with a word.
Yet the thread with which it is woven is so enduring
That miles from home a memory can reopen
An uncompleted element of discord,
And what takes place can be a painful curing.

To comprehend the puzzle of the Human Family
One must simply open eyes and take a peep.
Look within the fragile and invincible screens
Of your own family to explore the mystery.
It's there you learn – or do not learn, and weep –
What the phrase and concept "Human Family" means.

FRESH EYES

Wake up, you sleepyhead!
Get up, roll out of bed!

See everything anew.
It's within the realm of you.

To be awake, you realize,
Is to see everything with new eyes.

Make every time the first.
Repeat with fervent thirst.

Resist comparing from before;
Look freshly and see more.

If beauty and wonder make you quake,
Then you are truly awake!

FORMULA FOR JOY

If you want joy, more joy in your life,
Here's the secret of attaining it:
Do what you're doing with more joy — enjoy!
Or, as the Nike ad says, "Just do it!"

How do you behave when you're joyful, at play?
Got it? Okay, now behave that way!
What are your thoughts when you're joyful? It's a test!
Whatever it is, think them now, with zest!
How do you feel when you're joyful? Are you reeling?
Then feel it — feel that wonderful feeling!

Your joy begets a cycle of joy.
You reap whatever you sow.
So do things with joy, with love and compassion,
And your life will be all aglow!

PLAYTIME

Sometimes you get so caught up in your days
That time runs out for you to take a break.
There's lots of time ahead for you to work,
So listen up and learn, for heaven's sake!

In spite of what your mind is telling you,
It's safe to take some time for you today.
It's good to fuel your creativity,
So make free time for you – and simply play!

Play tickles the child that nestles deep within –
The one over which you try to have control.
It's safe for you to take the time to play,
For play's the thing that always nurtures your soul.

LIFE'S LESSONS

POLARITIES, PARADOXES, AND PUZZLES

Many of life's lessons are simple,
Straightforward, honest and true.
But just for fun, or maybe for ornery,
Some try to confuse me (and you?).

Take this, for instance, I've read somewhere
That all behaviors contain
Their opposites. How can that be?
(I think I'm getting a migraine!)

"Hyper-inflation leads to collapse."
"What goes up must come down."
"You must be generous in order to prosper."
(On my brow there is a frown!)

"The feminine outlasts the masculine."
"He" causes while "she" allows.
"The feminine surrenders, then encompasses, and wins."
(How's that for raising eyebrows?)

And finally, "The water wears away the rock;"
"And spirit overcomes force."
"The weak will always undo the mighty."
(To this, one says, "Of course.")

The lesson here is to always look
For more than meets the eye.
Learn to see things from all angles.
It's easy if you try.

HUMILITY

A grateful heart is the beginning of greatness.
It is an expression of humility.
It is the foundation of all the virtues:
Like courage, contentment, happiness and nobility.

Humility is not thinking less of yourself;
It is thinking of yourself less.
It's not doubting your powers or holding your tongue,
But knowing what's right and acting with thoughtfulness.

Humility is becoming a lost art, it seems,
But it is not difficult to practice each day;
And it begins by realizing that others have been
Involved and helping you along the way.

Maya Angelou said it well: "There are people before me.
I've already been paid for and {in my wisdom}
I must prepare myself so that I can pay
For someone else who is yet to come."

MAGNIFY THE GOOD

When encountering others in your daily living,
Always magnify their attributes, not their mistakes.
And compliment them for what they've achieved.
Be positive, be helpful, for heaven's sake!

Because, what you allow to occupy your mind
Will magnify in your life without fail.
We are what we think about, all day long.
It depends on the thoughts we allow to prevail.

The more you think of the good fortune you have,
Be it health or friends or enough to eat...
The more good fortune will come to you.
So magnify the good and life will be sweet!

START FROM WHERE YOU ARE

"Of course," you say, most incredulously,
"Where else would one start from anyway?"
You'd be surprised at the amount of time
People wait for conditions to be okay
Before springing to action on the rest of their lives;
Before starting on the road to make things happen.
Don't wait until you think conditions are perfect.
The opportunity to move on doesn't come that often.

Start where you are and use what you have.
You'll gain more as you continue to move.
If you stand still, the world will pass you by.
But as you progress, conditions will improve.

Motion is where your ideas will come from.
You are your own rhythm section as you continue your way.
Your dance of life will move effortlessly
As you pursue your endeavors with an attitude of play.

Explore and thrive, always challenging yourself
To greater and higher participation as you grow.
Don't sit idly by, watching the world whirl past.
Be alert. Join the dance. Be the flow.

PERSEVERANCE

"It does not matter how slowly you go
As long as you do not stop."
Confucius uttered these words of wisdom...
A philosophy that you should adopt.

Continuous effort – not strength or intelligence –
Is the key to unlocking your power.
Your potential is disclosed to you and to others.
It's a most wonderful adventure.

You may encounter many defeats in your life,
But you must not be defeated.
The setbacks only serve to make you stronger.
Your efforts must be repeated.

Many of life's failures are people who gave up
Just short of achieving success.
"Never, Never, Never give up!" shouted Churchill.
His wisdom about perseverance is limitless.

Life is not easy, but so what of that?
Perseverance and self-confidence are needed;
And believing you are gifted for something to attain...
Your success to you will be speeded.

Perseverance is not a long race, you see.
It's many short races in a row...
One after the other, step after step...
Until you've arrived at the "show."

Success is owed to perseverance;
No one succeeds without effort.
The secret of success is constancy to purpose.
Disraeli said this in his report.

BELIEVE

Everything is always impossible
Before you actually succeed.
"Impossible is just an opinion!"
Make this your undying creed!

Believe that your life is worth living.
It will help you create that fact.
Sometimes things have to be believed
To be seen... and have an impact.

Never let what you cannot do
Interfere with what you can.
It's impossible for you to fail
If you believe and follow your plan.

Your faith is the daring of your soul
To go farther than it can see.
Every day, miracles are possible.
With that, you must agree.

It's not who we are that limits us,
But who we think we're not.
Luck is believing you're lucky.
So, give it your best shot!

POWER OF YOUR THOUGHTS

Thoughts create substance; they're the basis for all
That we are, that we have, that we see.
Marcus Aurelius said, "Everything is
That which we think it {to be}."
And Emerson... that's Ralph Waldo himself...
Found himself in a position to agree.
He said, "You become what you think about
All day long." He's right, you see.
"All that we are is the product of what we've thought,"
Says the Dhammapada with no irony.
And Buddha said, "All that is is the result
Of what we have thought." ...same repartee.
"Make the most of yourself, for that's all there is
To you," Emerson said, profoundly.
Your thoughts reign supreme, you create it all!
Ask the experts... that is their theory.

FROM GANDHI

It's all in the mind, it's how we see
Ourselves without input from others –
Whether free and nice looking or in bondage and unsightly,
Choose the positive – you do have your druthers.

Freedom comes NOT from somebody else.
It comes from one's own resolve.
The fears, when one takes a stand for one's self,
Have no choice but to dissolve.

Freedom and slavery are mental states.
The fetters fall when one resolves to be free.
The moment one mentally frees one's self,
Life changes. That's a guarantee!

HOW TO BECOME AN ADULT

We stay forever stuck
In all the psychological muck
About our parents' raising,
Or lack of proper praising:
"She didn't bake me cakes!"
"He didn't like my snakes!"
"She spanked me when she shouldn't!"
"He wanted to hug, but couldn't!"
No matter what our upbringing,
It's woes we're often singing:
"They didn't do it right!"
"My life is just a fright!"

To get past feelings of anguish
We must be willing to relinquish
The past and all its pain,
And get on with our lives again.
Forgiving our parents doesn't mean
We agreed with their whole scene,
Or supported their behavior
As anything superior.
It simply means we're willing
To make our lives fulfilling;
By making the present last,
And letting go of the past.

ON BEING SCARED

It really is okay to be scared.
It gives courage a chance to come into play.
You can do your best things when you're a little off-center.
You work from mystery and not knowing the way.

"Courage is being scared to death,
And saddling up anyway," said John Wayne.
The risk of a wrong decision is preferable
To the terror of indecision. Oh, the pain!

Fear is the unknown; it's what you do not know.
Courage resists it and overcomes it's pull.
Fear makes strangers of people who could be friends...
People with whom a friendship could be delightful.

And hate, to go one step further, is the consequence of fear.
We always fear something before it turns to hate.
Your life shrinks or expands in proportion to your courage.
Knowledge is power. You must investigate!

It really is okay to be scared
And fortune favors the one who has courage.
Fear makes the wolf bigger than it is.
With courage you have the distinct advantage.

LIVE A LIFE TRUE TO YOURSELF

The most common regret of people nearing death
Is lamenting the lack of courage
To have lived a life being true to themselves.
(Those who do have a decided advantage.)

Living your life that others choreograph,
If not true to your own dreams and wishes,
Is no life at all – no matter how posh.
Your life is your own to establish.

The choices you make will guide your life.
By honoring your dreams you stay true
To yourself and to others who are in your life.
Being true to yourself is a virtue!

FROM GOALS TO ACTION

To plan before one leaps off into action
Makes sense. Losing time is such a waste.
If going over your mistakes seems redundant,
Try planning before rushing off in haste.

A goal is called a dream with its own plan.
It is hard copy of projected thoughts.
And though it may evolve as time goes on,
The goal keeps us on track for our best shots.

Our wasted effort is reduced by much,
And ordered lives allow us to do more.
Our action is inspired by valid plans.
Success upon success is ours to score!

LOOK TO YOURSELF

To look at another person's talents
And envy them for their accomplishments
Is to waste the golden opportunity to
Hand them their well-earned compliments.

The time you spend envying their success
Could be better spent on preparing for your own.
We each are given special talents at birth.
Discover yours; build on your own cornerstone.

Your irritabilities and frustrations run rampant
When your creative powers are wasted.
There is possibly nothing so disappointing
Than your desired successes untasted.

We all have our own very special talent.
Some of us are blessed with more than one.
Act on it, hone it, make it work for you.
If you don't, you'll lead a life without fun!

When you wish you could be like someone else
You give over your power to another being.
You move farther away from realizing your own.
Look to yourself, and love what you're seeing.

EMOTIONAL HONESTY

Santayana had such wise, wise thoughts.
He is quoted often in 'sound bites.'
His wisdom applies to everyday living;
His words are sparse, whet the appetite.

'There is no cure for birth or death,
Save to enjoy the interval,' he said.
The pathway to your 'cure' might be
To follow your heart and your head.

'The young man who has not wept is a savage,
And the old man who will not laugh is a fool.'
Emotional honesty at any age
Should be part of the Golden Rule.

LIFE'S GIFTS

SERVICE

If you've ever wondered why you're here
Please listen closely, have no fear.
I'm about to share some words to revere.

You came for service, to volunteer;
To help others on earth within your sphere;
To ease their burdens, to blot a tear.

To carry your own load, to persevere,
To be of help, any time of year;
To not take lightly, to be sincere.

The rent we pay for being is dear.
It's service to others, the purpose is clear.
It's not "part-time," it's your career!

LET YOUR TEARS FLOW

Rejuvenating, purifying, and salty they come –
Tears, beautiful tears, so clear and wholesome;
They carry light-bearing power as they flow;
They cleanse our soul's windows and relieve our woe.

The Hermits, the Mystics, the Spiritual Beings
Learned of the power of tears. They were seeing,
As they watched people crying, a change in their faces –
A kind of renewal, a vision of grace.

"Old Ones" favored highly the "Gift of Tears."
Crying is recommended for those in all spheres.
Just as the rain precedes the rainbow
So does weeping precede the light of the soul.

BEING PRESENT

Deep living requires presence in your whole being...
In the present, in the now, I must impart.
Don't hang onto the past, or dream of a future;
Move into your body and you move into your art.

Cast off what doesn't serve you... old tapes, old habits.
Ask your body to guide you throughout your days.
Accept the part you play in causing your problems.
Learn from it and focus on changing your ways.

Your job is not to determine life's meaning
But to discern it... there is a big difference.
Know that you don't know, then get on with your life,
Staying centered with minimal interference.

It's said that no matter the problem, the answer
Is to meditate; go to your safe underground.
It's a secure place to go to, a kind of retreat.
When times are problematic, results can be profound!

Inner peace aligns you with the more positive aspects
Of your own personality, and it shifts you
From grandiosity to grandeur; from littleness to magnitude,
And you can live in the way of "to thine own self be true."

It's all up to you because it's all inside your head.
Move to bring head, heart and body all together.
Then your creativity can prosper, you're free to explore
All the beauty and talent inside you, in any weather.

IF YOU CAN'T BE THE ROCK, BE THE RIPPLE

You may think you have no power to change things;
But, in fact, you do, and here's how:
It takes but one person, one moment, one conviction,
To start a ripple of change somehow.

Each time you stand up for a noble ideal,
Or act to improve the lot of others in your scope,
Or strike out against any injustice,
You send forth a tiny ripple of hope.

Everything is purposeful; it changes the way you live.
Everything you do has a ripple effect.
Every word you utter, every action you take,
Affects other people and the planet. (That's correct!)

When you drop a new idea on the pond of the world
A ripple effect begins immediately.
You have to be aware that your idea will create
A cascade of change for all to see.

People will talk about wanting to change things;
To help and to fix the world's woes.
Ultimately, all you can do is fix yourself.
A ripple effect follows, the solution grows.

SELF INTENTION

If you accept your thoughts as facts
Then your road to discovery is blocked.
You assume you already know everything,
And your mind will be sadly locked.

You must be willing to challenge all aspects
Of your life, and its contents, it's true...
Including your reality. You may be reaching
For things that aren't right for you.

There are no accidents in this life.
Of course, you knew that in advance.
So, live your life with intention, because
Authenticity does not exist in a life left to chance.

YOU HAVE THE POWER TO CHANGE THINGS

The single greatest power you have
Today is the power to change some things.
If what you see is out of whack
Then you must pull some "altering" strings.

It would be grossly irresponsible for you
To let it continue as status quo.
Change is required in order that
We all will have a better tomorrow.

All existence is in a perpetual flux
Of being and growing into something new.
That's what is known as evolution;
There are times that change depends on you.

DREAM BIG

To dream big, my friends, is a matter of choice.
To reach it is a matter of discipline.
Dream big, work hard, and never stop believing
That all is possible. Go within.

If people say you dream too big,
They actually are thinking too small.
Dreams always come a size or two larger
So we can grow into them, that's all.

Dream big, you are an Infinite Possibility.
You will become what you believe.
Create the grandest vision possible for your life.
You'll be thrilled with what you'll achieve!

And if it offends someone, dream bigger!
If their nose is out of joint, that's tough!
If people aren't laughing at your dreams,
Then your dreams aren't big enough!

Don't call it a dream; call it a plan,
Then go forth with courage, it amuses.
Success occurs only when your dreams
Get bigger than your excuses.

SUCCESS

Success requires that you get up
One more time than you get "decked."
Getting knocked down, and then getting up
Is part of life... a fact that can be checked.

If you stay down, you miss half of life...
The half that makes the whole worthwhile.
Life isn't perfect, it can seem unfair,
But it beats the alternative by a country mile.

Great strides and big splashes are not necessary
To gain the respect you desire from your peers.
Show a willingness to get up and try again,
And you will know success, my dears.

Life may throw you some really hard tests,
And you may say, "It doesn't seem fair."
But be consoled in knowing what you get
Is an opportunity to get somewhere.

Turn what you learn into useful information,
Then come back even stronger than before.
Self-pity is defeating, and so is fear.
Play the game; you'll gain even more!

The task is hard, there is no doubt.
The secret of triumph is to pay your dues.
It's hard, alright, to "win the bet,"
But it's even harder if you lose.

TAKE CARE OF YOURSELF

I was having a conversation the other day
With a friend who shared this sentiment:
"If anyone else treated me the way I do,
I'd have to kill that person." (An acknowledgement)

So, why is it, why do we leave
Ourselves to the very last?
We care for others, our lovers and mothers,
But treat ourselves as though outcasts?

To stay grounded, I read a terrific idea:
Use pumice on calluses, a little each day.
It puts us more in touch with the ground,
And it makes the unsightly things go away.

Just because it's raining, or snowing or blowing,
Doesn't mean we can't build our strength,
And stay toned and aerobically fit for life.
Be willing to go to any length.

And weight can and will take care of itself
If emphasis is put where it belongs...
On eating healthy and avoiding the rest.
(Dieting and fasting are for "ding-dongs.")

And lastly, the body can heal itself
Of nearly all things that can ail it.
If caught in time, the miracle is rest.
The word is sleep. You must do it.

CARPE DIEM

If you want your life to be a magnificent story
You must first realize that you hold the pen.
Each new day provides you with opportunity
To write a new page the way you've chosen.

Each day's a new day, so seize it and live it!
The future starts today, not tomorrow.
Each day comes bearing gifts to be untied.
Don't ever look at what you've missed with sorrow.

Live daringly and boldly and fearlessly today.
Right now is all that you have, for sure.
Now is the time to make a difference.
The time is now. OK, you get the picture.

A CLOSING THOUGHT

POETRY

It's the revelation
Of a sensation
That the poet
(Wouldn't you know it)
Believes to be
Felt only interiorly
And personal to
The writer who
... **writes it.**

It's the interpretation
Of a sensation
That was fueled by
A poet's sigh
And believed to be
Shared mutually
And personal to
The lucky one who
... **reads it.**

About the authoR

Kathryn Carole Ellison is a former newspaper columnist and journalist and, of course, a poet.

She lives near her children and stepchildren and their families in the Pacific Northwest, and spends winters in the sunshine of Arizona.

You might find her on the golf course with friends, river rafting, traveling the world, writing poems... or enjoying the Opera and the Symphony.

Late bloomeR

Our culture honors youth with all
It's unbridled effervescence.
We older ones sit back and nod
As if in acquiescence.

And when our confidence really gels
In early convalescence...
'We can't be getting old!' we cry,
'We're still struggling with adolescence!'

Acknowledgments

I have many people to thank...

First of all, my amazing children—Jon and Nicole LaFollette—for inspiring the writing of these poems in the first place. And for encouraging me to continue my writing, even though their wisdom and compassion surpass mine... and to my dear daughter-in-law and friend, Eva LaFollette, whose encouragement and interest are so appreciated.

My wonderful stepchildren, Debbie and John Bacon, Jeff and Sandy Ellison, and Tom and Sue Ellison who, with their children and grandchildren, continue to be a major part of my life; and are loved deeply by me. These poems are for you, too.

My good friends who have received a poem or two of mine in their Christmas cards these many years, for complimenting me on the messages in my poems. Your encouragement kept me writing and gave me the courage to publish.

To Kim Kiyosaki who introduced me to the right person to get the publishing process under way... Mona Gambetta with Brisance Books Group. I marvel at her experience and know-how to make these books happen.

To Amy Anderson, Sonya Kopetz, Kerri Kazarba Schneider, and Ingrid Pape-Sheldon, my very creative public relations team of experts, who have carried my story to the world.

And finally, to John B. Laughlin, a fellow traveler in life, who encourages me every day in the writing and publishing process. John, I love having you in my cheering section.

BOOKS OF LOVE
by Kathryn Carole Ellison

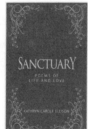